Kenya

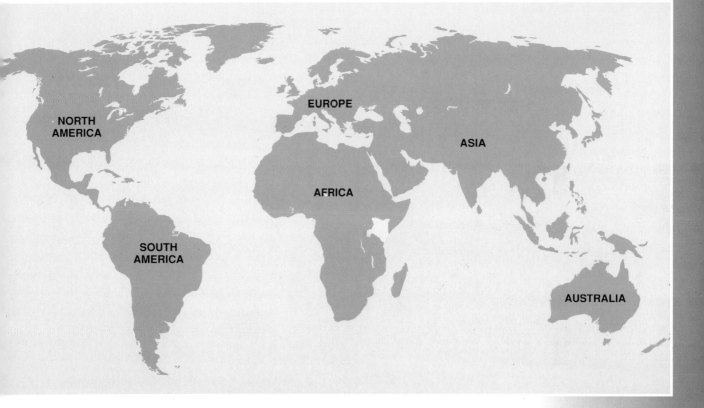

Fred Martin

First published in Great Britain by Heinemann Library
Halley Court, Jordan Hill, Oxford OX2 8EJ
a division of Reed Educational and Professional Publishing Ltd

Heinemann is a registered trademark of Reed Educational and Professional Publishing Ltd

OXFORD FLORENCE PRAGUE MADRID ATHENS
MELBOURNE AUCKLAND KUALA LUMPUR SINGAPORE TOKYO
IBADAN NAIROBI KAMPALA JOHANNESBURG GABORONE
PORTSMOUTH NH (USA) CHICAGO MEXICO CITY SAO PAULO

Designed by AMR
Illustrations by Art Construction
Printed in Hong Kong / China

02 01 00 99
10 9 8 7 6 5 4 3 2

ISBN 0 431 01369 1

WORCESTERSHIRE COUNTY COUNCIL	
620	
PETERS	10-Sep-99
J916.762	£9.99

British Library Cataloguing in Publication Data

Martin, Fred, 1948-
Kenya. – (Next Stop)
1. Kenya – Geography – Juvenile literature
I.Title
916.7'62

Acknowledgements
The Publishers would like to thank the following for permission to reproduce photographs:
Aspect Pictures, Peter Carmichael, p.23, Tom Nebbia, p.8; Hutchison Library, Timothy Beddow
p.25; Link Picture Library, Sue Carpenter, p.19; Panos Pictures, Jeremy Hartley, pp.4, 26, Betty
Press, pp.5, 24, 29, Sean Sprague, p.14; Planet Earth Pictures, Sean Avery, p.6, Roger de la
Harpe, p 10; Still Pictures, Adrian Arib, pp.18, 28, M&C Denis-Huot, p.9, Mark Edwards pp 11,
22 Fritz Polking, p 7, Hartmut Schwarebach, p.15, Trip Photo Library, p.12, 13, 16, 17, 20, 21,
D. Saunders, p.27.

Cover photographs: Robert Harding Picture Library and Gareth Boden

CONTENTS

INTRODUCTION TO KENYA

Kenya: towns and population

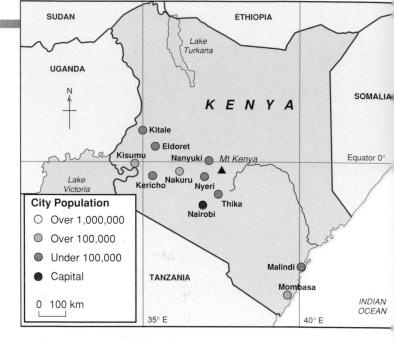

Kenya's ancient history

Human skulls that are at least five million years old have been found in Kenya and in other parts of east Africa. Some **anthropologists** believe that these belonged to the first people to walk upright and to make tools.

Different tribal groups in Kenya have developed their own civilizations over many centuries. Some tribes **migrated** from other parts of Africa. The Maasai people, for example, moved into the area in the sixteenth century. These groups sometimes fought with each other, but they usually lived their own way of life in their own tribal areas. There are about 70 different tribal groups. The main group are the Kikuyu people.

Celebration day.
- *A group of schoolgirls celebrating Kenya's Independence Day.*
- *The flag shows Kenya's national colours with the shield and two crossed spears.*

Independent Kenya

Kenya was ruled as a colony by the British for about 70 years. It became an **independent** country in 1963 after a long fight for freedom by the black African people. A year later, it became a **republic** with its own president. Kenya's flag shows a shield and two crossed spears as a reminder of the country's different tribes.

Kenya gets its name from the country's highest mountain, which is called Mount Kenya. This name comes from its Kikuyu name of *Kere-Nayaga* or *Kirinjaga*, which means 'the mountain of whiteness'. Although it is on the equator, the mountain is so high that there is always ice and snow at the top. In 1849, a German explorer named Ludwig Krapf became the first European to see Mount Kenya.

A growing country

Kenya is among the world's poorest countries. It is known as an **economically developing country (EDC)**. The population of just over 28 million is growing so quickly that it may double in the next 30 years. This growth is both a cause and a result of the country's increasing problems of unemployment and poverty.

People need children to help with farm work and to look after their elderly relatives. But when too many people try to farm the land this can destroy the country's natural vegetation and soil. These problems sometimes make people disagree with each other in a way that leads to violence. There were riots in 1997 when students and others protested against the government.

A daily chore.
- *Women and their children fetching water from a pump.*
- *Clean water from a tap would be a luxury to many people in Kenya.*
- *The population in Kenya may double over the next 30 years.*

In 1899, a famous geographer named Halford McKinder became the first European to climb to the top of Mount Kenya.

5

LANDSCAPE

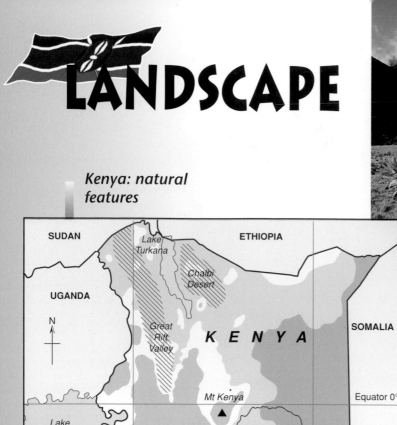

Kenya: natural features

The peaks of Mount Kenya.
- *The peaks are always covered by snow and ice.*
- *There are glacial lakes called tarns in some of the mountain hollows.*
- *The dark volcanic rock shows that this is an old volcano.*

Volcanoes, active and extinct

The **relief** of Kenya is divided into areas of mountains, hills, plains and coastal lowlands. The highest mountain is Mount Kenya at 5199 metres. Most of the mountain is the remains of an extinct volcano. The hard volcanic ash and lava have not yet been worn flat by the weather. The Menangai Crater, at a height of 2490 metres, is more evidence of Kenya's old volcanoes. Some of the volcanoes are still **active**.

Active volcanoes are situated along a crack in the earth's thin outer **crust**. This runs through Kenya from north to south. Lava and other volcanic materials sometimes pour out through the cracks or through craters. This forms a deep and wide valley with steep sides called a **rift valley**. The Great Rift Valley is up to 80 km wide in some places. The steep sides are called **escarpments**. The Mau escarpment rises for about 3000 metres from the valley floor. It is about 320 km long.

Highlands and Lake Victoria

There are highlands with hills and valleys on both sides of the Great Rift Valley. In the far west, there is Lake Victoria, the world's biggest freshwater lake, situated on a **plateau**. Only a small part of the lake is in Kenya. The larger parts are in Uganda and Tanzania.

The largest rivers in Kenya flow eastwards from the highlands to the Indian Ocean. The Tana and Galana rivers are the biggest of these. Many rivers in the north only flow for a few months. They dry up in other months because of the lack of rain.

Plains and coast

The land becomes lower and flatter towards the east and the north. In the south, there is a lowland coastal plain that is about 100 km wide. The Nyika Plain in the north, towards Kenya's borders with Somalia and Ethiopia, is much wider.

Kenya's coastline along the Indian Ocean is 536 km long. There are beaches with fine white sand. This comes mainly from broken pieces of the **coral reefs** that lie offshore.

Lake Turkana in the north is the largest lake completely in Kenya. It is 6405 square kilometres (km²) in area, 394 km long and varies between 16 and 32 km wide. Rivers flow into it, but none flow out again. This is because it is in the Rift Valley and it is lower than all the surrounding land.

The River Mara.
- *The river flows through the Maasai Mara National Reserve in the south of Kenya.*
- *The surrounding landscape is an upland plain.*
- *Trees grow on wetter ground along the course of the river.*

CLIMATE AND VEGETATION

A tropical climate

Apart from the mountain tops, nowhere in Kenya is cold during the day. In the north, the daytime temperature can reach 40°C, falling to about 20°C at night. On higher land further south, the average monthly temperature is between about 16°C and 18°C. The equator passes through Kenya so it should be hotter. It stays cooler because of the uplands.

The average monthly temperature reaches a peak twice in a year. This occurs because of the tilt in the earth's axis. The sun is high in the sky in two different months.

Seasons and rain

The northern areas are much drier than those in the south. This gives a landscape that is **semi-desert**. Rain in the south falls mostly when the weather is hottest. Scattered cumulus clouds form as warm air rises, but rain from these clouds is very unreliable. Sometimes giant thunderclouds build up and there are torrential downpours that only last a short time. There are about 250 days with thunder over the Kisii highlands near Lake Victoria.

A herd of impala in the Amboseli National Park in the south of Kenya.
* *Scattered trees and grasses grow in the savannah landscape.*
* *Scattered cumulus clouds do not bring any rain.*
* *The mountain is Mount Kilimanjaro in Tanzania.*

In the Maasai Mara National Park there are about 1.3 million wildebeest and about 250,000 zebra.

Big game country

The greatest number and variety of plants and animals are found in the wetter areas in the south. These areas are grasslands with scattered baobab trees and acacia bushes. This is called a **savannah** landscape. The grasses grow to several metres high when it is wet, then die down when it is dry. Fires are often started by lightning. Some species are fire-resistant so they can survive. Less than three per cent of Kenya is covered with forests.

The amount and variety of Kenya's wildlife – both large and small – are hard to count. Hippos, crocodiles and birds live in the lakes and rivers. On the plains, there are herds of gazelle, antelope and wildebeest. There are smaller numbers of elephants, giraffes and hunting animals such as lions, cheetahs and leopards. Birds of prey such as vultures and eagles also live there.

Large areas called **game reserves** and **national parks** have been set up to protect the wildlife. One problem is that having too many animals in an area can destroy the natural environment. Keeping big animals such as elephants away from people's farmland is another problem.

A herd of wildebeest.
- *The herd crosses a river on the annual migration to grazing lands.*
- *Crocodiles sometimes attack the wildebeest in the river.*
- *People can easily see the zebra's black and white stripes against the colours of their natural background, but lions and the other 'big cats' only see in black and white.*

9

WORLDS APART

Moving homes

Three out of every four people in Kenya live in small **settlements** in the countryside. In the north, tribes such as the Rendile and the Somali people are **nomadic pastoralists**. They move their herds of camels and goats from place to place to find grazing land. When they move, they dismantle their homes and take them with them.

The houses have wood frames with straw and leather sections for the roof and walls. Barriers of thorns are put around the huts for protection against wild animals and thieves. This nomadic way of life is dying out as the population increases and there is not enough land left to allow them to move about.

Village people

Village settlements are different in the south, where farming people such as the Meru and Taita stay in one place. They build groups of round huts, using a wooden frame with walls made from mud, twigs and cattle dung. The roof is made from straw or corrugated iron.

For the Maasai, each group of huts for a family is called a *manyatta*. The family is an **extended family** that includes aunts, uncles and other relatives. Villages have become larger in recent years as the country's population has increased.

Making a home.
- A Maasai woman spreading cattle dung on the roof of her house to make it waterproof.
- The frames of the huts are made from sticks and poles.
- The walls are made from straw and mud.

Houses in Nairobi.
- *People from the countryside build their homes from scrap materials they find in the city.*
- *Wealthy Kenyans live in comfortable houses with electricity and piped water.*

City life

Most of the **urban** population live in either Nairobi, the **capital city**, or in Mombasa, the main port. There are only two other towns with populations of over 100,000. Most other towns are local **market towns** with about 5000 people.

Nairobi is one of Africa's fastest-growing cities. In the centre, there are wide streets, modern office blocks, cafés, houses and shops. Politicians and business people have meetings at the Kenyatta International Conference Centre.

Most people in Nairobi live in **shanty town** buildings they have built themselves. Most shanty town districts are on the edges of the city. Some people build homes wherever they can find an empty piece of land. About three-quarters of the homes in Nairobi have been built illegally on land the people do not own. Many shanty town dwellers grow their own food and keep livestock.

In 1899, a railway camp was built at a Maasai watering place called Enkare Nairobi. This was along a railway route that was being built between Mombasa and Uganda. By 1905, the new town of Nairobi had become the capital city of Kenya.

LIVING IN THE CITY

The Mutisia family

Machakos is about 80 km east of Nairobi. This is a built-up area with a town centre and large areas of housing. One of the biggest housing estates is the Buru Buru Phase II estate. About 10,000 people live there including Mr Muunda Mutisia and Mrs Jennifer Muunda. They are married and have two children. Mike Muunda, the oldest, is eighteen years old. His brother Samuel is fourteen years old. They have a fourteen-year-old maid to do the housework, the shopping and the cooking.

The family outside their home in Machakos.
- *Samuel is wearing his school uniform.*
- *There are also big blocks of flats in Machakos.*

The family live in a house with two bedrooms, a sitting room and a dining room. The house is made from brick with a roof made from tiles. The floor is cement. There is a kitchen with a gas cooker and a kerosene stove. The family buy their gas and kerosene from a petrol station. There is a garden where the family grow vegetables. They keep a fierce dog to protect their home from burglars.

This is the living room in the family home.

A maid is cooking a meal for the family.
- *She is using a gas oven.*
- *She often cooks rice with vegetables and meat in a stew.*

A day at work

Mr Mutisia works as an accountant for an insurance company in Nairobi. He drives to work every morning, leaving home at 6.40 am. There are always traffic jams on the roads in the morning when he goes to work. Jennifer Muunda travels to the Nairobi City Market where she sells **craft** goods.

Mr Mutisia likes to play sports and keep fit. He plays football and table tennis for his company. Jennifer keeps fit by going to keep fit classes.

Learning

Both the boys are still at school. Mike goes to a secondary school. Sam goes to the Bidii Primary School which is near to where he lives. There are up to 48 children in each class. Sam goes to extra lessons after school. He wants to do well in his exams so he can go to boarding school in Nairobi. He knows that a good education will help him get a good job.

- *Mr Mutisia at work in his office.*
- *He uses a computer.*

- *Jennifer has a business selling carvings.*
- *Many of the carvings are of animals in Kenya.*

13

FARMING

Living by farming

About eight out of every ten people in Kenya work in **agriculture**. It is hard to make a living by farming where the rainfall is unreliable and there are often **droughts**. With more people in Kenya, there is less land for each person. Growing more food on less land can ruin the soil.

Maasai farmers herding their cattle.
- *This is the traditional way of farming for the Maasai.*
- *Maasai farmers now also grow crops.*

Animals and crops

In the **semi-desert** areas in the north, farmers are mostly pastoralists. They rear herds of camels, goats and cattle for milk and other products. People sometimes drink or cook with the animals' blood, for iron and vitamins. The animals are too important to be killed for their meat. The herds are moved from place to place to find fresh grazing land and water.

In the southern highlands, the Bantu people farm on land called a *shamba*. Each family has their own small plots where they grow maize, millet, vegetables, cassava and bananas. Chicken and goats are other sources of food. The Maasai used to be cattle herders but now they grow crops as well. This is because some of their grazing land has been taken to use as **national parks** and **game reserves**.

Subsist or sell

Most farmers live by **subsistence farming**, which means that their family eats most of what they grow. When they need new farmland, the men clear away trees and bushes. The rest of the farm work is done by the women. Moving on to new plots when the old ones are exhausted is called **shifting agriculture**.

Families often work together to help each other. It needs everyone in a village to build a dam and dig water channels for an **irrigation** scheme, or to build stone walls to stop soil erosion. The government is trying to get more farmers to work together in **co-operatives**. This should make it easier for them to grow more and sell produce to people in the cities.

Some crops such as sugar cane, tea and coffee or flowers are grown as **cash crops** to be sold. This is called **commercial farming**. Cash crops are sometimes grown on large farms called **estates**. This is how the British used to run their farms in Kenya.

Coffee and tea are commercial crops, but two-thirds of the coffee and half the tea are grown on small, family-owned farms.

The tea crop.
- *Picking tea on an estate.*
- *The tea is exported to earn money for Kenya.*

LIVING IN THE COUNTRY

Mangu school and village

The village of Mangu is about 35 km north from Nairobi. The village is beside the Mangu High School. There are only 100 people living in the village. Most of the adults work for the school. Mrs Veronica Wangari Kamande is a school cleaner. She also helps with the cooking and looks after sick children. Veronica has seven children. Four of them go to school and one works as a maid. Her oldest daughter, Lucy, is married and her oldest son, Zacharia, works as a groundsman for the school.

- *Veronica inside her house.*
- *There is a curtain to divide the one room at night.*

The school has given Veronica some land where she grows crops. She grows maize, beans cabbage, bananas and a fruit called paw paw. The family eat most of the food but they sell some to the village shop.

The family home

The family live in a house that has one room. This is where they cook, eat, do their homework and sleep. The ground is an earth floor. The walls and roof are made from sheets of corrugated iron. The room fills with smoke when the meals are being cooked. This is a nuisance, but it helps keep mosquitoes away.

- *Patrick, aged ten, is lighting the fire to do the cooking.*
- *The cooking is done using firewood.*

A classroom in the village primary school.
- *There is no door and no glass in the window.*
- *Vegetables are grown in the school grounds.*

There is only one fresh water tap in the village.

Firewood is used to do the cooking. The children have to collect the firewood. The pots quickly go black because of the smoke. There is no electricity in the village but there is a supply of fresh water. This comes from one water tap.

For entertainment, the children sometimes play football or watch television in the school.

The primary school

Veronica's youngest children go to a primary school nearby. This is the Kurahia Primary School where there are 600 children. John Gikonyo is one of Veronica's children. He Is twelve years old. There are no doors or windows in the school. Parents have to pay a small fee every term, but many people are too poor to pay it. It is very hard for Mrs Kamande to pay for all of her children to go to school.

Patrick, John and a young friend with their pet rabbits.

17

BUYING AND SELLING

Market days

Most people in Kenya buy the things they need from street markets. On market day, women walk to the market carrying small amounts of farm produce for sale. Some carry their goods on their heads. They set up a market stall on the ground along the roadside. They spend the day under an umbrella to shade them from the sun. Selling vegetables and other food helps them to pay for clothes, cooking equipment and their children's school fees.

Factory goods

In the past, almost everything was made by the village people. Cloth, farm tools and pots were made by village craftsmen and women using local **raw materials**. Now people can buy plastic buckets, T-shirts and bottles of Coco Cola. More goods are **mass-produced** and less are made by hand. Many of the **manufactured goods** are imported from countries such as China. This is because there are not many factories in Kenya.

As people make less, they need more money to buy what they need. There are also changes because of better transport to and from the cities. This makes it easier to bring more factory goods to the countryside. It also makes it easier for farmers to sell farm produce in towns and cities.

Market day in Kenya.
- *A busy market scene in Lotokitok.*
- *Food, clothes and all types of goods are sold by the traders.*

Buying clothes.
- *A shop for women's and children's clothes in Nairobi.*
- *Most shops are small though there are also some big department stores in the city centre.*

City shopping

There are local street markets in every neighbourhood in cities such as Mombasa and Nairobi. There are also some larger and more specialized markets. In Nairobi, for example, the City Market sells cut flowers and baskets woven from a crop named sisal. Making these baskets is done as a **craft** industry.

Most local shops are small with shelves stacked with tins. Food is sold in tins because most people don't have fridges to store it in.

There are modern smart shops, including department stores, in Nairobi. There are shopping malls and plazas where high quality goods are bought by the few in Nairobi who can afford them. Some of the most expensive goods are made by hand such as hand-stencilled fabrics. The mass produced factory goods do not have the same appeal as the more unique products made by hand.

Visitors to Kenya used to buy wildlife skins. Selling these skins is now illegal so that the animals can be protected.

19

EATING AND DRINKING

Banana trees.
- *People eat what they grow.*
- *Bananas can be added to many dishes.*

Food from crops

People who live in Kenya's farming areas mainly eat the food they grow themselves. A typical Maasai meal would have boiled maize called *ugali*, eaten with a meat or vegetable stew. The maize is ground or pounded into flour before it is cooked. The Pomoko people eat rice and plantains they grow near the River Tana.

Green bananas are steamed, mashed or boiled and added to a meat or fish stew. Cassava is another **staple food**. It is grown where the rain is most unreliable. Beer and spirits are made from crops such as millet and maize.

Food from animals

Some people depend on their animals for food. They get milk from their cattle, camels or goats. The milk is drunk fresh, made into butter or the curds are eaten.

The diet of the Somali people includes honey from wild bees. They only eat meat during special ceremonies or when an animal becomes old and dies. People who live near rivers and lakes are able to catch and eat fish. Nile perch from Lake Victoria can be up to two metres long, more than enough for a full family meal. Shrimps and oysters are caught along the coast. Buffalo steak with wild honey is on the menu for tourists in some **game reserves**.

Some tribes have customs and religious beliefs that do not allow them to eat some types of food. The southern Nilotes, for example, are not allowed to eat fish.

Cooking problems

Finding water and firewood for cooking is becoming a problem in Kenya. Women fetch and carry water and firewood from many kilometres away. This takes time and is very tiring. This problem is getting worse as the country's population increases.

Traditional food stores are round huts made from mud and straw. These do not keep out insects, nor do they keep grain free from fungi. The result is that much of the food is ruined. Metal storage bins are one answer to this problem.

On average, people in Kenya get 2075 calories from their food every day. This is very much below the world average of 2718. People in the world's richest countries usually take in about 3300 calories every day.

Cooking a meal in a hut.
- *Wood has to be collected to make the fire.*
- *Some people use simple cookers that burn kerosene.*

21

MADE IN KENYA

Craft goods

Kenya is not an industrial country. Many people make goods in their homes using traditional **craft** methods. They use local **raw materials**, such as wood and clay, to make tools and pots. Some craft goods, such as jewellery and leather goods, are made to a very high quality.

Goods are also made in small open workshops called *Jua Kali*, which means 'hot sun'. Tools and pieces of equipment are made from pieces of scrap metal taken from old cars and other pieces of broken machinery. Plastics, tins and car tyres are also **recycled** to make new products. People in Kenya are experts at doing this.

Factory goods

Some goods are **mass-produced** in factories. Crops, such as sugar cane, tea leaves and coffee berries, are **processed** to make sugar, tea and coffee. Beer and other alcoholic drinks are made from crops and honey. Farming also supplies the raw materials to make clothes and leather goods. Sisal is grown to make baskets.

Trona is a mineral found in Lake Magadi in the Great Rift Valley. It comes from hot mineral water that comes from volcanic rocks underground. It is mainly used in washing soda, baking soda and soda ash.

An open-air workshop in a **shanty town** district of Nairobi.
- Workers are making metal goods, such as beds, window frames and boxes.
- Goods are often made using scrap metal.

Factory work in Kenya.
- *Women in a factory making prints on cloth.*
- *Factory methods are used to mass-produce the cloth.*

There are some **heavy industries** such as making cement and glass. Imported crude oil is refined in Mombasa to make petrol and the chemicals that are used to make plastics. Most other **manufactured goods**, such as cars, are imported from industrial countries such as the UK and Japan.

Making wealth

Kenya is among the world's poorest countries when measured by its **gross national product (GNP)**. This is the value of everything that people produce in a year. On average, each person produces only $270 worth of goods. This is just under 70 times less than people produce in the UK or Australia.

People in Kenya will not find it easy to become more wealthy. There are almost no raw materials, such as metal ores, or **fossil fuels** such as oil or coal. It is also hard to start a new business when most people do not have much money.

Only seven out of every hundred people work in factories. Only about 20 per cent of the country's wealth comes from manufactured goods.

TRANSPORT

Tracks and roads

People in Kenya walk to collect water and firewood, and they walk when they to go to school, a clinic or a **market town**. These places are linked by networks of local tracks and paths. It is not unusual for people to walk up to 40 km in a day.

There are 62,573 km of roads in Kenya, but only 8322 km are paved. The unpaved roads have potholes, mud, dust and shallow river crossings. They are only suitable for off-road vehicles such as Land Rovers. Heavy rain can make these roads impassable, even for off-road vehicles.

Most people in towns and cities travel on buses and in crowded minibuses named *matatus*. The main bus station in Nairobi is known by local people as 'Machakos airport'. Nairobi's roads are becoming very congested and dangerous.

A minivan in Nairobi.
- *There is not enough room for everyone to travel inside.*
- *Some goods are pulled on a cart.*

Long distance by rail

There is a skeleton network of rail services between the main towns and cities. There are only 2652 km of railway track in the whole country.

Mombasa is linked to Kampala in Uganda by a 1000 km railway line. From the coast, the line goes 500 km inland to Nairobi, reaching a height of 1616 metres. The overnight journey between Mombasa and Nairobi takes just under fourteen hours at an average speed of 35 km per hour. There are first, second and third class fares. The journey on to Kampala across the Great Rift Valley takes another 22 hours.

Air and sea

The fastest but most expensive way to travel is by air. The flight between Nairobi and Mombasa only takes one hour. Nairobi's main airport is the Jomo Kenyatta International Airport which was named after the country's first president.

Tourists, doctors and government officials often use light aircraft to get to more remote places. Airstrips are usually dusty and bumpy. A new way for tourists to see Kenya is by hot-air balloon. This is a perfect way to watch the wildlife without disturbing the animals.

Mombasa is the country's main sea port. There are also local ferry services on the larger lakes such as Lake Victoria. Most rivers are too shallow and their flow is too irregular to make them **navigable**.

The Mombasa to Kampala railway line was thought to be a mad idea when it was built between 1894 and 1901. This is why the line is sometimes called the 'Lunatic Express'.

Travel by train.
- *This train links the two biggest cities, Nairobi and Mombasa.*
- *The line was built about one hundred years ago.*

SPORT AND RECREATION

Time for sport.
- *Girls playing in a girls' school.*
- *Schoolchildren are expected to wear a uniform.*

Record breakers

Kenyan middle and long distance runners are among the best in the world. Kenya's first Olympic medal was won in 1964 when Wilson Kiprugut won a bronze medal in the 800 metres. Since then, athletes, such as Kipchoge Keino and Henry Rono, have won gold medals and broken world records at most middle and long distances. In 1978, Henry Rono broke five world records in 50 days. Some of the best athletes leave Kenya and go to run and study in American universities.

The success of Kenya's athletes has made many young Kenyans take up athletics and other sports. Football is already popular in schools and on the streets. Kenya now has a national football team that competes in international competitions. Basketball is another fast-growing sport with the national team taking part in international competitions. Children also play volleyball and netball at school.

Sports for some

Some sports, such as bowls, golf and horse-racing, come from Kenya's colonial past. These sports are becoming popular with wealthy Kenyans. There are only ten eighteen-hole golf courses in the whole country, although more are being built. Facilities for water sports and diving are being built along the coast to attract more tourists. However, it will be a long time before more than a small number of Kenyan people will be able to afford to take part in these sports.

Kenya is on the route of the East African Safari car rally and other races. These are long-distance races on both paved roads and unsurfaced tracks. Car companies use the race to advertise that their cars can survive these difficult conditions.

People at play

In Kenya there is a custom to enjoy yourself at the same time as you are doing something useful. A *harambee* is held when people want to work together or raise some money. People join in to help each other with singing, music and dancing.

Children in the towns and villages play the same simple ball games and games of tag that children play in most other countries. Perhaps one day some of them, too, will become international athletes.

The oldest golf course in Kenya is in Nairobi. It was started in 1906. Golfers say that a golf ball can travel ten per cent further than normal in Nairobi. This is because the air is thinner at Nairobi's high altitude.

On safari.
- *Tourists on a safari holiday in the Amboseli Game Reserve.*
- *Conserving wildlife is good for the tourist industry.*

CUSTOMS AND FESTIVALS

Children's work.
- *Children have the job of looking after goats and other animals.*
- *These children are milking the goat.*
- *When they are older, they can leave the village to take cattle to grazing lands.*

Local customs

About a quarter of Kenyans are Christian. There is also a small number of Muslims. These people celebrate events such as Easter and Id-ul-Fitr. Most people however, have their own tribal beliefs, customs and festivals.

These customs and festivals are important parts of everyday village life. The festivals are often to do with farming and hunting. Marriage is an important event to celebrate. For the Tharaka people and for most other tribes, a gift has to be given for a bride. A gift of five cattle or sixty goats is usually given for the first wife. For a second wife, the gift is only three cattle or thirty goats.

Special rites

Most groups have special ceremonies called **initiation rites**. These mark when a boy or girl passes from youth to become an adult.

The Rendile people divide people into different age groups, with special jobs for each group. The youngest boys help look after animals in the family compounds. When they are older, they leave the village and go to camps where the camels are grazed. As young men, they become part of the warrior group. After a few more years, they become members of the group of elders who make all the important decisions. The women have their own special jobs but do not take part in making the decisions.

Some initiation rites involve circumcision, or making other marks on the body. Others involve shaving off hair, and body painting.

Maasai men performing a traditional dance.
- *The dance is in a special village set up for tourists.*
- *Dancing for tourists takes away the real meaning of the dance.*

Singing and dancing

Dancing is part of many ceremonies. The Kamba people dance by jumping up in the air and performing acrobatics. Some movements show what warriors do during battles. The Maasai men dance by leaping high in the air. Maasai women are not allowed to do this. They have to keep in contact with the earth which is the people's source of food and life.

Many traditional beliefs and customs are under threat. This is because of tourists, radio and television and because so many people are moving to live in the cities. Some changes may be for the better. Others could make people lose their links with their tribe and their family.

Kenyatta Day, on 20 October, is a national day to celebrate the country's independence. It also helps bring the different people of Kenya together.

29

KENYA FACTFILE

Area 571,416 square kilometres

Highest point Mount Kenya 5200 m

Climate

	January temp.	July temp.	Total annual rainfall
Nairobi	18°C	16°C	958 mm

Population 28.2 million

Population density 50 people per square kilometre

Life expectancy
female 63, male 59

Capital city Nairobi

Population in towns and cities 25%

Population of the main cities (millions)
Nairobi	1.4
Mombasa	0.5
Kisumu	0.2
Nakuru	0.1

Land use
Grass	67%
Forest	4%
Crops	3%
Other	26%

Employment
Farming	81%
Industry	7%
Services	12%

Main imports
Machinery
Vehicles
Petroleum
Chemicals
Manufactured goods

Main exports
Coffee and tea
Petroleum products
Vegetables and fruit
Corn
Hides, skins and other animal products

Language
Kikuyu	20%
Luo	14%
Luyia	13%
Kamba	11%
Kalenjin	11%
Other	31%

Note: Many of the languages are local tribal languages. English is also spoken.

Religions
Christian	66%
Traditional African beliefs	26%
Muslim	8%

Money The Kenyan shilling (Ksh)

Wealth $US270
Note: This is calculated as the total value of what is produced by a country in one year, divided by the population and converted into US dollars.

GLOSSARY

active (volcano) a volcano that still erupts

agriculture farming

anthropologists scientists who study how people behave and change

capital city the city where a country has its government

cash crops crops that are grown to sell

commercial farming growing crops or rearing animals to sell

co-operatives groups of people who work together and share the profits

coral reefs barriers that are mostly underwater made from both living and dead coral

craft a traditional way of making something

crust the hard thin outer shell of rocks around the earth

droughts long periods without rain

economically developing country (EDC) a country where many people are poor and where farming and industry are being improved

escarpments steep slopes that run across the landscape in lines

estates very large farms that are run as businesses

extended family immediate family members plus more distant relations

fossil fuels fuels such as coal and oil that have been formed from ancient plant or animal life

game reserves areas where wildlife is conserved

gross national product (GNP) the total value of what is produced by a country in a year

heavy industries industries that make goods such as metals and ships

independent an independent country has its own government

initiation rites ceremonies to mark a change in a person's life

irrigation channeling water to crops

manufactured goods goods made in factories

market towns towns where there is a regular street market

mass-produced made in large amounts in a factory

migrated moved from one place to live somewhere else

national parks large areas set aside to conserve the natural landscape and its wildlife

navigable a navigable river is one that boats can use

nomadic pastoralists people who herd animals and move them from place to place

plateau an upland area with steep sides and a mainly flat top

processed something made from a raw material

raw materials the things that goods are made from

recycled made from materials that have already been used before

relief the shape of the land

republic a country with a president

rift valley a valley with steep sides caused by cracks in the earth's crust

savannah a tropical climate with a hot and wet season and a warm and dry season

semi-desert an area almost as dry as a desert

settlements places where people live, such as towns and villages

shanty town an area of houses that people have built for themselves around the edge of a city

shifting agriculture moving to new farm plots by clearing part of a forest

staple food the main food that people eat

subsistence farming growing enough to live on

urban to do with towns and cities

INDEX